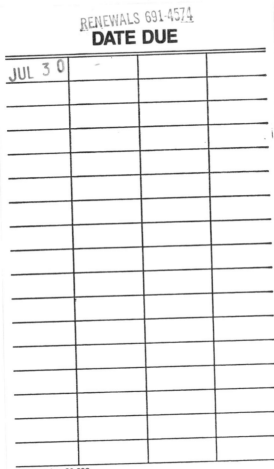

RENEWALS 691-4574

DATE DUE

JUL 3 0			

Demco, Inc. 38-293

A SEASON OF LOSS

A Season of Loss

Poems by Jim Barnes

PURDUE UNIVERSITY PRESS
West Lafayette, Indiana

Published 1985

Library of Congress Cataloging in Publication Data

Barnes, Jim, 1933–
  A season of loss.

  I. Title.
PS3552.A67395S4 1985   811'.54   85-3634
ISBN 0-911198-75-X

Printed in the United States of America

For Carolyn, with love

CONTENTS

I. BONE YARD

II. Dog Days

ACKNOWLEDGMENTS

Grateful acknowledgment is made to the following publications in which many of the poems first appeared: *Seven:* "Bone Yard"; *West Coast Poetry Review:* "Paiute Ponies," "Thunderstorm in a Nevada Ghost Town"; *Concerning Poetry:* "Halcyon Days"; *Beliot Poetry Journal:* "Near Crater Lake"; *Journal of Irish Literature:* "A Rannaigheacht Ghairid on Spring Burning"; *Nimrod:* "Song of I-see-o," "Odyssey"; *Long Pond Review:* "At the Burn on the Oregon Coast"; *CutBank:* "On the Mountain"; *Sunday Clothes:* "Right Place, Wrong Time," "Rabbits"; *The Nation:* "Postcard from Poison Spider Creek, Wyoming," "Four Things Choctaw"; *Mississippi Review:* "Trying to Hide Out on Rich Mountain," "Sweating It Out on Winding Stair Mountain"; *Saltillo:* "Choctaw Cemetery," "Black Mesa Nocturn"; *Southwest Review:* "Black Mesa Sundown"; *Interstate:* "Badlands Mirage"; *Poem:* "A Sunday Dreamer's Guide to Yarrow, Missouri," "A Song for All of Them"; *Dacotah Territory:* "A Season of Loss"; *Pacific Quarterly Moana:* "A Season of Sun Dogs"; *The Arlington Quarterly:* "Dog Days"; *Southern Poetry Review:* "Rest Stop at Horse Thief Spring"; *Three Rivers Poetry Journal:* "Return to The Roundup Tavern"; *The Laurel Review:* "The Long Lone Nevada Night Highway"; *Poetry Now:* "Yuma: The Greyhound Depot"; *Chicago Review:* "Notes for a Love Letter from Mid-America"; *River Styx:* "Sundays"; *Twigs:* "For Geoffrey Firmin, in Hell"; *Quartet:* "On Location at Tongue River"; *Georgia Review:* "Heartland"; *Prairie Schooner:* "Ghost Fog"; *St. Andrews Review:* "The Captive Stone"; *New Letters:* "Accident at Three Mile Island," "La Plata, Missouri: Clear November Night"; *Cimarron Review:* "5-Ring Circus at Season's End"; *Green River Review:* "Call It Going with the Sun"; *Rocky Mountain Review:* "The Sentence," "Autobiography, Chapter X: Circus in the Blood," "In Memory of a Day Nobody Remembers: September 26, 1874"; *Coyote's Journal:* "Crow"; *Kentucky Poetry Review:* "Parable"; *Agni Review:* "Toy Soldiers"; *North Dakota Quarterly:* "Decades," "Surviving the Storm"; *Texas Review:* "The Drowning"; *Poetry East:* "Dirge"; and *The Point Riders Great Plains Poetry Anthology:* "January Wind."

The following poems also appeared in *Carriers of the Dream Wheel: Contemporary Native American Poetry* (Harper & Row, 1975): "Sweating It Out on Winding Stair Mountain," "The Captive Stone," "Bone Yard," "Paiute Ponies," and "Halcyon Days."

"A Sunday Dreamer's Guide to Yarrow, Missouri" also appeared in *Heartland II: Poets of the Midwest* (Northern Illinois University Press, 1975).

A word of gratitude and thanks is due to the National Endowment for the Arts; without the 1978 Fellowship in Poetry, this book would not have been completed.

I.
Bone Yard

A word has power in and of itself. It comes from nothing into sound and meaning; it gives origin to all things.

—N. Scott Momaday,
  The Way to Rainy Mountain

A hundred buffalo
knee-deep in sludge.

Bones bleached to pebbles
and white sand.

No buzzard troubles
now to drop an eye
on long-spent bones
at this dried waterhole.

The land's cracked hide
speaks of thirst.
No tree lives.

Only the ghosts of hoofs
that still tramp along
play on a hot wind
which has no past.

Only in dead of winter
do the hoofs grow still,
when humped clouds
crowd low against the ground.

Silhouettes, they lean against a ringed moon,
their heads down against the threat of snow.
Below, a distant diesel moan runs
along the tracks, where dead coal cinders
gather frost, and plays out toward Winnemucca.

No movement. They hump against the night.
Only quivering patches of skin crack the air,
memories of a summer's fly.

Mane and tail hanging vertical as ice,
they sleep dead centuries,
or if ponies dream they dream.

Below on the flat where light strikes water,
a last ember sparks out. A dog complains.

The diesel warns again, begins its roar, passes.
They raise their heads like automatons, blink,
then drop once more into centuries or dreams.

For Dagmar Nick

Last night in La Plata an avalanche of stars
buried the town in constant light the way the red
coalburners on the Santa Fe used to send fires

climbing night and falling back again, burning sheds,
hay, carriages, whatever was set along the track.
An avalanche of stars, last night the Leonids

fired every farm with ancient light, curdled milk
in Amish churns, and sent dogs howling through field
and tangled wood. Never was there such a night like

this. Lovers sprang from one another's arms, reeled
away from lurching cars and thoughts into a state
of starry wonder no human act could have revealed.

As if by common will, house lights went out. The late
work left, families settled out into the snow
unaware of cold, unaware of all except that state

which held us all for those long moments. We saw
and saw again the falling stars course Bear and Swan,
take field and farm, take all, and give it back as though

a gift given was given once again. Our lawn
on earth was full of promise in the snowing light.
Earthbound, we knew our engine on a rare November run.

Charlie Wolf used to whittle skinning knives
and swords from empty apple crates in winter.
He carved out blades I knew would never break,
true blades I knew instead would slice right through

any weed I chose to make a running deer
or any Rhode Island Red I chose to see
as enemy of God and man. Each old hen
knew my whoop meant feathers lost or worse

and squawked accordingly. Old Charlie used
to say that's why we got so many eggs
double-yoked—"scared the stuff right out of them
with that sword and that wild-eyed Choctaw yell."

Every sword I ever had before Charlie
drowned drunk on a coon hunt on the Arkansas
smelled of apples. Streaking round the barnyard
junk like a bullsnake after chicks, I breathed

pure Christmas before each ambush of red hens,
the white pine sword gleaming between my teeth.

Between hill and river the trail
forks, edges deep in stone only
shadows know, and only the stones
can say which way my fathers took.
Steps and lives have worn away
the mountain agates' chalky maps
so I can say they went this way
or that and knew the sounds upon
the land, knew too the rush of wings.
The hill fork leads to a sky beyond
the hill, the river fork down water
fast with rainbows and quick jacks.

Ways my fathers walked are things I
learn from hard stones. I lift my arms
and hold the bear, the bull, the lost
maidens, and the hunter mad for game;
I make a prayer for the drawn bow
to send beyond the sun and down
the last dark corridor of sky:
old fathers, when you come again,
old fathers, tell me once again
why the path forks and the river
runs fast with fish to homes beneath
another sky, homes beneath the sea.

The horses know a rain turns quick to flood
north of Winnemucca and shake their hides
in a leaky lean-to rattling in the wind.

The gulch that cuts the Cattleman's Paradi off
from what may once have been the madame's house
begins to run like lobo sin
straight to Yaqui Chihuahua.

My wife tells me there are bottles at the rear.
I watch a spider take a desert fly
too dry ever to have heard thunder.
Stained, deep purple bitters bottles:
she lines them on the ratty bar.

We came for relics, not the deep red water
we watch claim the morning's tumbleweeds
and spent lead from range war .45s.

The drink we take from canteens wrapped
in Hong Kong wool is Himalayan tea, we pretend.
We wait until the gulch goes by. Dry, we ride on.

Slowly, smoke
settles in the hollows. Poke-
weed grays, cinquefoil withers, jack-
in-the-pulpits crack. Frogs croak.

The woods ring
alive with the fire of spring.
Though the flame may kill first plants,
no rants are raised at burning.

Rather now
in this cool time of hawk, owl,
and hummingbird—acceptance
of the balance due to fowl,

beasts, creatures
of the leaves and grass. Features
of ash give way to the force
that will course fields and pastures

with a green
that will outlast the first seen
things of the small woods and ways.
All the days of spring we keen

being slow,
loss of faster things. We know
so little the force of fire:
death here, we say, should grow slow.

I have watched the changeless mountains receive the sun.
I have seen the prairies black with the trampling buffalo.
I have heard the wild, dark cries in winter's hungry wind.
I have tasted the sweet and flowing water of the Quohada plains.
These things I have done, and I am glad to be a man.

I have counted the ageless stars in the Moon of Falling Leaves.
I have sought in troubled dreams the other side of the sky.
I have lived to see the prophecies of Maman-ti come to pass.
I have known the hot anger of Satanta and Gui-pah-go.
I have ridden through the Moon of Going Geese with Tay-nay-angopte
And my heart rides on to Rainy Mountain, my heart rides on.

I have watched the changing prairies receive the sun,
And I remember plains where grass was tall as man.
I, Tahbone-mah, have lived the old ways and the new.
The loneliness of the plains, the boredom of adobe walls.
These things I have done, and I am glad to be a man.

No more shall I race through nights of the Big Leaves Moon.
Before the Moon of Buds is down my spirit will pass
From this my mouth and ascend to the Great Milky Way.
But my heart rides on to Rainy Mountain, my heart rides on.

---

*Born Tahbone-mah, later called I-see-o. Died March 11, 1927.
Kiowa warrior and later army scout under General Scott. Keeper
of one of the great Kiowa sacred medicines.

Maman-ti, Satanta (White Bear), Gui-pah-go (Lone Wolf), and
Tay-nay-angopte (Kicking Bird) were Kiowa chiefs.

In the Days of Many Horses, for the Kiowas and Comanches,
Rainy Mountain and Rainy Mountain Creek in southwestern
Oklahoma were sacred and favorite camping places where the
grass was always green and the buffalo plentiful.

In Memory of a Day Nobody Remembers: September 26, 1874*

Who is left to recall the sacred earth
where Poor Buffalo bit the dust?

The dance of days is the only dance.
Town Indians drunk on Chock and Thunderbird

can never know they were born of a hollow log
or the ritual of the sacred sun dance doll.

Nobody can recall the massacre
of men, and horses dead in Tule Creek.

The racial memory fades. O son of man,
what anvil hand forged your soul and skin?

Isatai, who promised to vomit bullets
at Adobe Walls, would have you dance again.

Or Maman-ti, who willed the death
of white-tongued Tay-nay-angopte.

Exploded bones fuse with sand. No grass grows.
Of the chinaberry trees, just one or two.

Palo Duro Canyon: echoes also fade.
K'ya-been's bones lie buried in the bluff.

Dance, ghosts, among the yellow leaves
before they turn to dust.

---

*On the night of the 26th, Colonel Mackenzie and his troops from
Fort Sill attacked the camp of the last freedom-loving Kiowas and
Comanches, killing Poor Buffalo and several others. No soldiers
were lost. The next day, the cavalry slaughtered between 1,000
and 1,400 Indian horses near the mouth of Tule Creek.

From the low
cracked clouds this clocking wind
turns the fresh snow stone

and lovers
to their beds where the cover drifts
like undulating dunes.

In this cold
time, wind is law, relentless force,
that you cannot coerce.

You judge
the wind by standards not your own:
reeling planets, the sun

falling out
of sight, even the long wobble
of the earth, its spindling pole.

Harbinger
of death and a stillness time cannot touch,
the wind does not instruct.

Nonetheless,
you feel that the January wind
knows the in and out of things.

The hills' heads lie bodiless on the mist,
ghost ships deadlocked on a ghostly sea, masts

rigid and dark against the faint ashen light of dawn.
Among last trees, the ringed fingers of sun are slow to sound

the depths of gimcrack trunks. The flagged trail
wakes to the wayward gamming of jays. The last wail

of an owl sinks away: the night bird battens
down fast against the day. Now the running wind

wafts through the crossed bones of trees and beasts, quick
as needles to thread the hills together, to stitch away the dark.

The hide is nailed
upon the door.

The old bitch strains,
licks a sore forepaw.

The pup trails asleep,
hounds a first
wild hunt into
his hell of dream.

A low wind
lifts the dust
up off the floor,
inches it
toward the fire.

The pup runs
a spastic course,
freezes and bays
himself half awake.

The wind dies down;
the fire sparks out.

The old bitch groans
herself to sleep.

The hide is nailed
upon the door.

You have noticed that the truth comes into
this world with two faces.

—Black Elk, an Oglala Sioux

At Lame Johnny's hanging,
they say
one old left-over Sioux
got drunk
& started a racket heard
beyond Hermosa.

He sang & whooped a circle
round the tree
like some goddamned witch on holiday.

He prayed
in four directions, kissed the horsedunged earth,
counted clouds,
& summoned up his grandfathers' ghosts.

They say he sang
it to the world old Lame Johnny's one eye
got big as a buffalo's,
the other the size of a rat's.

He prayed
all day, while Lame Johnny danced,
& circled round & round
what they say he called the sacred tree.

Dear wife, space is momentary to the mind,
someone nearly said or wrote. I cannot
remember poems. Road maps have webbed out words,
but the feel of landscape here makes shutters click
even at 70 plus. There's something strange
about other places makes you want to
get where you never have to be: that point
you marked at sunrise. You watch the purple
turn to brown and marvel that all the creeks
are dry. Mostly you are afraid to stop,
and if you do you look for what you know:
your eyes are cameras that filter out the real.

Ruins have raked this mountain down to bedrock.
There's a lizard here quick as lightning
in the creek. Unique. Alone. So too alone
once this castle's ruins. Restored. Don't litter.
One year's life the great inn had before it
fell like dusk when all the Dutchmen went away
praising Wilhelmina, the old queen, her rusting
bones. You are here in soberer times. The green
mountain reeks of rotting moss and fresh crap.

Forty years you've lied yourself a life,
and now the woman that you love this late
knows all the barstools in the state, knows them
as you know these turned stones torn ragged
by a Caterpiller's track. The day opens
on your hot cot. You think you've fooled her
with this phoney suicide. She knows you were born
to cry. A lizard on your foot burns you
with a stare. The day opens wide enough to love.

Weekend tourists out of Tulsa sing
their beer cans empty. Four more beers they'll gun
their heavy cars down to Hot Springs sauna bars
and hear hard rock about mountains they will
never have to climb. The day stays open.
Wide. Wide as all the skies your forebears watched
eagles in. You wonder if you'd know their kind.
But it's too hot to pray Indians out of stone.

1.

Nashoba. This my father taught
me how to sing: Wolf, I look long
for you—you know to hide your scrawn-
y hide behind the darkest wind.

2.

Isuba. Horse: not one less than
twenty hands and all fast as hounds
with foxes in their eyes and off.
*Chahta isuba cheli.** Once
Choctaws bred horses not many
winds could catch. Listen: isuba
still races winter's darkest wind.

3.

Baii. Notice the oak, the high
white bark, the heavy leaves, how they
fall. Winters are long in mountains:
springs freeze at the source and wind bows baii.

4.

Abukbo. The feather that all
my life I sought beyond the sun.
I have fashioned a sacred shaft,
smoothed it red with wet clay and poke.
The feather will guide its arc down
skies where grandfathers walk the woods
quick with game, heavy with the wind's wild mint.

---

*Fast Choctaw horse

Stones,
hand-hewn symbols
touching
four winds.

Familiar glyphs:
*ushi holitopa.**
The dates:
short years.

Pollen settles
down on quickened stones,

and from the east
a distant roll of thunder.

*beloved son

A single-shot .22
and steady hand
could make you king
among the beasts
or ashamed to face
the checkerplayers
who were too old
to beat the field.

You killed because
you loved it
still; they crowned
kings reluctantly,
spat between cracks.

You could not know
the checkerboard
held acres
and each move
was deadly as
a hollowpoint.

You shot rabbits
until you lifted
the last one by the ears
and found a brain
checked, crossed
with a thousand moves
a rabbit had to take.

Clouds bruise
the hill beyond
a flint-strewn mound.

A painted sky
is best at red.

To count this sundown
you'll need more
than broken stones

and at your back you'll know
the icy moon and spinning stars.

Here the wind is a bad witch from the north:
beans and tumbling stones, sheep and hogans,
grip the earth when sand blasts adobe raw.
Leaving Santa Fe is no mean task. You
steel yourself against an afternoon of ease,
feeling a new grit forced into your guts.
The last pueblos know the wind better
than any tourist can.

               The museum
you came to see sits alone, saddling
the hill. Its hogan-dome inside climbs
to an apex you feel a star is raftered in,
a light for those who remember to look
up. Days are fierce within this wind
that spirals around the hill and through town.
There's something about the plaza that smells
of a gone and still unacknowledged sin.
The good Bishop lingers in the pink skin
of adobe walls.

              You hear spiders pray
as the wind touches bells that do not sound
and doors to the cathedral forever locked
against a night that's bound to arrive on time.
Hope lies in the absence of wind, in jambed
lives of tourists ogling nickel silver
and strings of plastic beads. Wally Whitedeer,
flat-assed and sweating under cameras,
counts dollar bills between gusts and reckons
he will buy that horse Samson Sorefoot tried
to gyp him on. That's his dream a weekend
in advance. Then the pueblos will ring with
horses hoofs and bells he'll put on the pommel.
Five dollars, he intones in Hopi drawl.
The tourists move along to Janey Feather's
belts. He'll lower his price on beads and smile
when the sun sinks into the softer earth
and the wind begins to lie.

                     In the heart there is
a pounding. In the heart of Santa Fe
the drummer drums because he wants a dance
no one knows the steps to. His beat strikes
the clock above the plaza and minutes jump
off cracked hands the Tewas know mean exactly
nothing: the ultimate no one disavows
who draws this hard Mexican air.

                           Mountainward,
the April snows begin to melt. Somewhere
the horses toss their manes and neigh into
the twilight of someone's ancient gods. In red
light the neon adds a gilted glare.

                              Galeria
del Sol features *An Afternoon of Rest*,
a portrait of a reclining woman muffled
in her dress, and for a modest fortune
she is yours to hang beneath a cross. Why
you are here and about to leave is something
you cannot know when the wind is native.
Twice in nine months you arrive in Santa Fe;
twice you leave, with regret you cannot name.
You are here to read your work to faces
lined by wind and red earth. You do not know
the angles of this land nor what the wind
hides from the hands that have summoned you.

A last ember
sparks quick
and dies.

You hum, hum low,
to see
if the ground
is real.

The eagle-bone whistle
lies cold
about your neck.

You count the cold light
of a hundred stars.

And you know you'll sleep,
sleep.

The sun against this butte
burns black earth back
to salt and slate

and ghosts of deer
track down from stars
brittle as spun glass.

Echoes in brilliant light
burst into being.

A buck bruises a pine
to velvet
where you know
no pine is

and does
are dozing
in its shade.

for Brian and Sharon Bedard

The town is tilted toward the stream,
oblique as shadows toward twilight.
But only the stream is on the move.
No wind to shake the rusty leaves
off trees that have never known a spring.

Standing on the bridge, you think the town
a creeper, some gray vine, thirsting
after a force to drive it home
into the hill.

                    And on the hill
all the houses are asleep, or dead.
Rainbow Bread is basic metal now,
and Stamper Feeds has only ghosts
of gears. You want a flight of birds.

Yarrow was once a flowered town:
you think of mint. There is no one
to ask, no one to tell you now
where forebears lie.

                    There are echoes
you are afraid to hear. You look
hard into the water and put a leaf
lightly against an eyelid to see
who is in your thoughts. A vision
dances on the skin: it is you,
the dancer and the dance.

                    On the hill
a last fresh grave blooms prismatic
in its finality.

We left the horses in the draw
and climbed the painted ledge to see
the blue and distance home but saw
an autumn sun set fire to trees

on ridges we had yet to pass:
gnarled trees that burned and stood
more than a shifting phoenix, cast
in colors other than mild moods.

Our blood was now too thin to know
the half-moon brother, our skin too pale;
yet we, hands out, tried again to sow
our spirit in the stars. A frail

effort: our fathers' blood pulsed slow.
At our back a glyph grew perfect:
hard in stone a hand drew back to throw,
a sun stood still, a moon arced, sticks

grew into bones. Only human,
we touched thoughts, hands, eyes,
assured ourselves of the moment,
and leaned together hard against the sky.

Hills where my father hid the bones
lie dark about me. I look for
trails hacked hard in trees and lined
in stones all years war with. I am
here this one night to find the farthest
corner of the sky, to place my body
one with earth, sky, to talk with ghosts
long silent, long dark. The turtle
is running through the tree, the flint
knife is shadow forced into stone,
the feathered snake holds hard in clay.
The way clear I can remember,
signs my father drew in the dust.
Hands know, hands talk. I salute the sky,
breathe quick hunters, slow bears, maidens
fleeing hard brothers and red shame.
Bones beneath my feet, I make
a song for all of them. My name,
earth name, is sacred as the sun.
My name goes with me out of this world.

For days you never see the sun,
always expect the worst. Double
or nothing. You write next of kin.
The sky is lead, and will not melt
even under a sun going
down double. The clouds hide stones;
the sun dog predicts a snowy
doom. Best to stay indoors and pray.
Word is out as far as the hills:
blizzard is much too mild a name.

You listen for the wind and try
your charms against the heavy north.
A voodoo doll might end the dread,
but north of Baton Rouge it wouldn't
work. The only hope is rain from
the Gulf, soft with the down of geese.
You send your soul away: say "take
it" to a friend who's heading south.
Cornfields as far as you can see
die flat under the weight of iron air.

A silent sun dog laps around
a cloud. You believe the two suns.
You have no choice. The ground beneath
your feet becomes another world,
one you know you don't know and can't.
You say a word, try to normalize
the lie. Nothing works, again. You
slit your eyes against the keening wind,
plan dirty jokes for cards, tell yourself
things change and hope the hell they do.

II.
Dog Days

*L'ardeur en secret, l'adieu
à la vérité, le silence de la
dalle, le cri du poignardé, l'en-
semble du repos glacé et des
sentiments qui brûlent a été
notre ensemble et la route du
chien perplexe notre route.*

—Henri Michaux, *La Lettre*

Hidden passion, farewell to
truth, silence of the stone, scream
of the stabbed man, all frozen
dreams and burning emotions have
been our lot, and the dog's road
confounds our road.

I dread the sultry August when days get short
and shadows long creep out to the mountains of the east,
when the dance of heat is seen far down the road,
when rivers no longer run but squat like turtles in their scummy houses.

For it is then that the dog trails my shadow,
his swollen tongue dragging dust,
a growl hidden behind filmy eyes;
when I stop, he stops, half within my shadow;
when I move, he moves, in step.

I dread the sultry August when days get short
and the sun seems a ball of fire-froth,
slithering from the jaws of the rabid beast
of sulky summer days
and my shadow lengthens and the dog is there.

The air is thin enough to make you cry
for home, and sounds among the cracking stones
ring of rattlers and long-dead horses' bones.
The military crossed here first, then horse
thieves walled the spring and stayed to build
a stone corral and die. A grave is opened
every year and all stones turned up for gold.
The laughter of dead mouths is keening in
the wind. Like waves, the thud of hoof on stone
never dies. A crow is drinking from the spring.

Three thousand feet above the valley's floor,
you caw the carnivore away and taste
his wild flight in water as old as sin
and cold as nights under this winter sky.
You hear the horses' breath, their frantic leap,
their rage to know the prairie far below.

Let them turn stones. Or tourists piss
in springs. Miles away from woman and sleep,
you know this sky is full, this earth alive
with sounds it will take you long days to hear.
You give five minutes more: to dream an ambush
and a hanging as heavy as this mountain's back.

The roots around your soul and eyes
after too much bourbon twist sockets
sore. This mountain's too high to cry
sober on, the sky too wide to fill
a brain. Three crows are wheeling
up a peak. Caws crack thin air.
Sweat ices its way down your spine.

Last night love loomed as lonesome
as a timber wolf, the face a mask
you painted in your drunken dream.
What's real is that one white, brittle
moon you think you see pied against
the coldest blue a summer has known.

Nearly forty years and you've yet
to learn that love is measured by
the sun. There's no shade. The wind
pulls at your hair. The sky burns black
at sundown. You've got to go back down
before the crows laugh you straight to hell.

for the Oregonians

Broken neon lariat and aging horse and rider
still signal sundown to street and S P tracks.
Sign and tavernfront are naked as the memory
of last Sunday's whore in Klamath Falls.
The building sags like some swaybacked mare
once swollen with life but now a ruined hulk,
grazing between the S P and the Mercantile.
The asphalt shingles curl like dead oak leaves,
into themselves. A blacked window reflects
the sunset.

          Silence sits like oil outside
the tavern. The street is half holes; the S P
goes black at dusk. The boardwalk sinks, creaks
of nails in fir. I pause at the battered door.
Inside, a lone shuffleboard player aims
a puck. The bartender dreams a fold-out.
There's an acid smell of piss and old pitch.

Silent as time, ghosts form in the shadows:
Tex glued to his customary stool by the tap,
elbows rigid, snoose juice streaming.
Old Pete, dead under a runaway S P car,
stands mid-bar. Big Ike, crushed under
concrete, raises one finger as if the act
itself were creation. Ivan lies stoned
on the perpetual floor.

          The battered door
is cold against my hand as the lone shooter
releases the puck and the bartender goes down
on an invisible page.

          From the Wurlitzer:
dead voices of Williams and Reeves and Cline.

Strangers we were friends for a long moment
on that long lone Nevada night highway
at the wreck (two dead on blankets or carcoats
on the gasolined pavement under our stars,
one other palely directing non-existent
traffic). He from the south, I from the north:
the long Nevada night highway is like that.
We both set our front-rear flashers working
and dug lone flashlights from stacks of states
and helped the dead, but did little for the other
till the trooper arrived (someone came before
us; he was known to us; he had stood here).

It was not blood or hard black pavement that
finally shocked us. These are commonplace.
Nor was it twisted metal, death, nor survivor.
It was only this: that after the taking
of numbers, after the siren's wail, after
the sanding of blood and the sweeping of glass,
after the conjectures, the sighs, the regrets,
what would there be to hold us to this spot
on the lone Nevada night highway where the stars
blanketing earth were ours and we were one?

Struck dumb by whispers
from the bed where I had
never been rocked, dumb from
my mother's return to him
from some far world, dumb from
her solid body not warming
the bed where we lay nightly
since I could remember arms,
save the forever she had been gone,
I heard their strange words.

In the wind-roofed loft above
my bed, rats rattled their quick
toes in that close tin hull
where night words went
to a final echoing rest.

Darkness surrounded me:
in my small vision, words
wasted in whisper rolled
like tiny scattered bearings
through the listing loft
no star shone on.
Words, silence, rats' feet:
the immense unending dark.

Somewhere beyond the reach of wind
I dreamed, dumb with knowing
she had come back to him,
that this beginning was the last
of something I could not name
in the vast inexactitude of youth.

In dull morning light
I woke to no memory of night, but
woke to the sounds of her slow step,
of wood and poker, of fire climbing
the tin stovepipe, and to her face
blue in the dawn room light
and the sheets trimmed and cool
against my cheek—and, O God,
it was something to be alive.

> *"Though nothing can bring back the hour*
> *Of splendor in the grass . . . ."*

—William Wordsworth

Then I never lost a song. Time was ever slow
and long. The grass flowed green to brown and back again
and I with it without reason except to sing
the silence full of sound the way the working wind
below the clouds found voice among the trees and low
of cattle grazing along the fence-rowed edge of field.

In my first decade the days bloomed wild with ravens
gamming brilliance, jays thieving, martins feeding quick
above our roof. There was no rain, no small neglect.
The immaculate skies did not portend a future storm.
All nights were warm, and innocence was there within
the house, the barn, the slow animals of our farm.

In my second decade I knew the war, of course,
which first loomed glorious, remote. Weapons I made
from empty apple crates. Then Time began to fade
into the shadows of my face: I could recall
yesterdays. My brother joined the Eighth Air Force.
I lost a dog. In those hard years, the first hard fall:

the weather taught me each could be the same—day,
love, war. Whatever I made a habit of
was deadly. And death did not end, only the brittle love
of first love I thought I'd not break through, then forgot
before the season turned. In that long, slow decade
I did not sing but flew the flag upon our lot.

In this whichever decade, my song comes slowly now,
the right sound seldom there, to catch Time where he is
or was and hold one moment in my hand, the chance
not guaranteed, but sought word on word, until
I hold a memory in light I'll surely know
and all the long loss of gone days is finally told.

A turquoise sky
low enough
to rub.

One bird,
maybe hawk,
a wing of light.

Somewhere,
a dog barks
silver as the night.

The smell
of a sin you can't define
in wind.

Years later
you will remember
only these of Yuma,
and a sudden pebble
in your mouth
will grow wet
against any desert
you have to cross.

On my desk is a cup which is empty.
I drank the last of the tea only a few moments back.
The cup is empty I say.
I want the cup full.
There is nothing to do with an empty cup.
I look for a tea bag.
There is none.
So strong is desire that my eyes water.
No tea in the world.
All cups empty.
I have died for the want of lesser things.

There is no death. Only a change of worlds.

—Chief Seattle

1.

No horizon promises a mountain.
Cornfields hide sparse trees
like snow the stone.

Mid-America in dead November
lies glacial
in the wake of this
a season come too soon.

I miss your eyes
in my eyes.
I miss my breath
in your hair.

A season of no promises
& a season of long regret:
we gave up our sense of place
for a sojourn in Mid-America
& you are gone in these
our elliptical days.

2.

We are happy in our mountains.
But roll them out
like unruled paper
& memory hangs like a pale woman
rocking on a wall.

Without a horizon
there is no land
worth the moment shared
when hills flung back
the best half of your name.

A sense of place
allowed us room to love.
No wonder salmon
take to falls.

I could die
where hills know
how to reach. Not here:
landscape will not allow
an *I protest*.

Wind breaks corn
that seldom sees the sun.

3.
Lost River. I remember it
by white-water sounds
& salmon mad with love
& rainbows dead,
rotting in the weir
my brothers made.

We swam the rapids
to love where moss
claimed rocks smooth with years.

You know the way it was all too well:
image is idea.
My eyes are full of you.

I will write runes
when letters fail.
For any part of you
that calls me fool
I'd give all mountains
I have left.

4.

But mountains do not last
where wind turns faces
hard as glacial drift.

Your name sinks
into the frozen offing

& only the taste
of crying it
hangs like an icicle
in my throat

& this alone I have left
from our sojourn in Mid-America.

I cross the river, the solemn bed of moss, the song of water over rocks.
The choir sings above the river sounds.
The stones and the river listen and the moss on the thrown skulls of fish.
All words are soft this Sunday.
Let us cloister this choir and resolve the disputes of the lost.
I do not know how anyone feels about war.
The stained glass throws haloes onto the pews.
The cross is falling, with all this light.
I am falling, falling into another solemn approach to the altar,
      that perpetrator of cold deeds.
I know still water runs deep over the dead skulls of fish, turtle,
      drowned man.
I alone listen to the choir of orphans.
Moss grows cold on the dark bark of trees and the detritus of night banks.
I can see the bottom of the shoal from the last pew and feel the presence
      of fishes and loaves.
The river confesses to the wind.
Only the fish listen through their one window to this other world.

¿Le qusta este jardin?
¿Que est suyo?
¡Evite que sus hijos lo destruyan!

—Malcolm Lowry, *Under the Volcano*

Below the garden on the hill
the barranca cuts through the road
and at the bottom lies a dog
rotting among old cars and dung
and grotesque masks from festivals
and traces of the Consul's bones.

And they have weathered long, these bones,
whose house had once loved well the hill,
loved well the fun of festivals,
and had at last walked down the road
to Parián with a sad red dog
to take his place among the dung.

Nothing now except bones and dung
remain to tell the tale; the bones
were not ferried across by the dog,
across the stream and up the hill,
but lie beneath the hill and road
amid Mictlan's dark festivals.

Tourists attending festivals
have often looked down at the dung,
while pausing whitely on the road,
and often wondered at the bones
but never guessed beneath the hill
a man was slaughtered, and a dog.

How horrible that reddish dog
then haunting Firmin's festivals,
constantly howling on the hill,
smelling of pulque and of dung.
A sack of skin with shivering bones,
it ate its puke upon the road.

And slanting down the Parián road,
the Consul sensed the shadowing dog
and felt the dread of death in bones
too tired for fear or festivals
above the barranca and dung
below the garden on the hill.

Now up the road I see a dog
and look beyond the bones and dung
to the festivals below the hill.

1. *Dream*

My father moves out of the dark
and touches me.
I sink away.

Bring light, he says.
There's something outside.

I push myself up on elbows,
full of dream.

I go through all rooms.
There is no light.

There's something outside, he says.
Hurry.

I go out without light
into liquid dark.

He is not there.
Nothing is there.

2. *To see the sea*

On the way we encounter storm.
The springy heather is leaden, gray.

The sea is over the hill, he says.
We're almost there.
                           Night falls.

The crows are silent, hidden.
Only the wind . . . .

And then the great gray mound of water
backed by cloud . . . .
There, he says, there is destiny.

My infinitesimal eyes strain against infinity.
I cannot see.
I hold tight to him against the wind
as the rain comes down.

3. *Requiem*

An aroma of wild mint.
People sing to flowers.
Brave boy, a hand on my shoulder speaks.

—Dust to dust,

The horses are bathing in the sea, my father says.
You will not see that often in this lifetime.

ashes to ashes.

The roses are wilted.
A dandelion bends beneath white stone.

Don't look at the sun.
It will put out your eyes—like that.

He is laid to rest.
Pray for his eternal soul.

Walk carefully into the night.
Let your eyes grow used to it.

A lone bird streaks skyward.
My eyes follow it.
The strange hand bites the bone of my shoulder.

The night the lights went out all hell broke loose:
a swirl of ghosts blew every other fuse,
the television burst, forecasted fate
rode wind and rain into another state
and left us sitting staring into the space
where all those years we'd fallen out of grace.

We watched the night as never before we had
as if something in the liquid dark were mad
and we were in for it, whatever the clouds
and balled lightning, furious roofs, and shrouds
of untreed birds could hurl our way. We prayed
into the brilliant dark as rafters buckled

like the deck on a rotting ship where doom
rode mast, bow, and souls of sailors gone dumb
with fear of falling into a maelstrom wide
as any Baptist view of hell. The side
of the house catching the brunt of wind bowed in
to the breaking point and snapped back again.

We smelled the hail. We felt something tornadic
in our joints. The roar of a billion bricks
breaking through took our ears. We could not speak,
nor did we dare to try. We knew the break
in wind would not come before our skulls cracked
and we descended breathless, damned by the black

sky, the relentless force that had willed this
all. We told ourselves we would never guess
that such a thing could hit, could dump us from
our chairs as easy as wind a feather or frond.
What mattered most was that the landscape freeze.
For that, and that alone, we bit our knees.

Certain death did not come. The hammering fist
pulled back, and the bellowing night grew still as mist
on moors. We unhinged our suppliants' limbs
as if they were fragile doors on ancient tombs.
We spoke to the night. We reconciled our fears
and with open hands reached for the light of stars.

My father's blood is strong: my bones grow hard with
      stakes in things and my veins pulse with a lively
      red from his nomadic ways.

There's a circus in my blood I've waited forty years
      to know, my father's hollow glance weighing on
      my shoulders like a sledge, his eyes gone blank
      under the sagging tent in dog days.

So here in this nonesuch bigtop in slow August, I
      surprise myself into a certain knowing. This
      thing is in the blood: a lust forever to move
      from place to place perfecting the one best act.

Henceforth I swear I will delight when I can name the
      earth new under my feet, keep my eyes clowned on
      where I am, and juggle my thoughts fast enough
      not to bore my ears.

And I will try to know the dancing in my blood, how
      it reels, steps, stops, and how on occasion it
      swings me out of tune, a dizzy fool whose brains
      are slower than his feet.

And I will praise my father for his shifting the shape of
      ways, for letting me know the permanence only of
      road; will praise my father and swing my heavy
      hammer to guy this my own ephemeral sky.

Half a town has grown
where you shot Goodman Two Cow
off his boulder horse
and started an uprising
you were Custer in.

You feel it's right
two slumping, feathered bucks
on painted pintos
cross the street

and the movie company man
grooms his beard with water
from a rusty turnip can.

You always knew they'd find
this place and make it
what it wasn't.

The scene grows stiff,
then dissolves into the game
you always played.

Who shoots first don't make a damn:
the important thing is falling.

The pintos reel away
and two bucks lie
giggling in the dust.

A crow calls from the ridge. Twice. Three times. I pinch my nose gently, cupping my left hand over the bridge of my nose. I caw the way the sawmillers taught me. I am a fool to think I can fool the crow. I caw. Twice. Three times. I see the black wings settle softly in on limbs high above my head. I never knew it would come to this. How I continue the conversation is exactly the point in question. Like an idiot, I put my hands in my pockets and stretch my arms with senseless glee. The crow preens his feathers, gives me sidewise looks. He drops like lead to eye level. The low limb twangs. I can see the world behind me in his black pupils.

From the rock
she dived into the shadow of herself,
and, hurling

the surface
into rainbows, her form split the mirror
of all forms,

and some god
held her long, too long for breath once held.
Her lover

woke slowly
into death's dream, calling as one might call
another

at dawn to
wake into a day in which each vista, distant,
is flooded

with first light.
She did not return, her fair form held deep
down below.

Her lover
moaned, endured, and still the water
held her form.

We could not
free her from the slow shadows that she palely
quite became.

Though we tried
our eyes and skill, nothing came up with our breath
      but a faint

      taste of lilies
and our curses against the play of light and shadow
      down among

      the gripping
depths that held her silent, still, and we turned
      our curses

      on ourselves,
and, as the water blazed us back odd voices, our eyes
      chiseled at

      every stone.

The houses die, and will not die.
The force of walls remains. Take
the family portrait hanging oval
on the wall and, underneath it
on the chifforobe, a dish of mints.

There are houses that fall, but their
shadows stay, lightly against a summer's
dusk. And there are photographs that
show ghosts of mothers walking halls,
of fathers fiddling in moonlight.

Even in disrepair, there's a life
to the houses. The rush of wind stirs
a soul: footfalls on wood and stone,
the creak of kitchen door, the last
words of a son gone away to war.

The houses die, and do not die.
There is something that will not let
a space be given solely to grass.
The aura holds, the center will
not fold, forever framed against
the graying sky, the coming night.

*I heard an Indian singing behind a rock pile. I
stopped and looked. It was Poor Buffalo. He
said that it was a great honor to be killed by
an enemy, and that K'ya-been already was
asleep.*

—Mumsukawa, a Comanche

At false dawn a dirty fog rolled up through
my camp on Tule Creek. On the first low wave
rode the heavy smell of a prairie dog town.
Then with full flood tide surging into the mesh
of my sleeping bag came earth-born, sky-bound
smoke of ancient campfires: Palo Duro Canyon:
the trill of an eagle-bone whistle, summoning,
the flap of a sacred owl-skin shaken high,
and Maman-ti's prophecies from the shadow world.
All stuck to me like red Texas mud. I dared
not move. I had scratched for horned obsidian
among K'ya-been's bones high up the canyon wall,
and the spidery hole moaned deep, forbidding,
and those webbed sockets branded me *Neuma-taker.**
The sun had made me brave.

      But now in this
dark dawn I thought I knew how it had been:
hunted, there they had still been free to choose
a place to die, to choose a place to die.
A hundred years flowed back and I was there:
Poor Buffalo has gone to sleep, his mother said,
my life is broken. And she wailed, wailed.
Shadow world.

     Then out of the pitch black west
a low and rumbling thunder set me straight.
Here was now: a trucker, damn his tunneled eyes,
barrelling-ass down the Amarillo-Lubbock run.

---

*"Eater of human flesh," a Comanche term of contempt for Tonkawas.

at Heavener, Oklahoma

Enmeshed in steel stands a stone,
near stunted ash and elm, cracked bones
of Yggdrasil, small trees of time:
the caged stone with ciphered runes
is part of Park where men once made
their mark with maul and biting bronze.

The aged stone, hard to hand's touch
when touch was still allowed,
has had its face forced clean:
lichen lies dead below washed runes;
webbed shadows of encircling steel
now mark time on the lone stone;
yet the stone stands as stone stood
when Odin still was king and came
with men to mark down lives and fates.

Now we who Sundays look long
on this stone's stark ruined face
see only stone and ciphered runes
under the steel's sharp shadows:
the whispering of wind through wire
carries scant legend, no hint of history.

Like a midnight eye, the hollow moon
opens wide against the empty jar.
The drumming light falls on leaves, on stones,
on the woman in white beginning to fill
the jar.

The hollow moon is laying down
a plan still a long way off.
The light that falls is all around
the woman and the jar. The woods are
enough

for the woman at the jar, and the moon
is enough. Its hollow light fronds
the trees like a summer storm. And soon
the woman will have filled the jar
and gone.

And the moon will have dropped into and beyond
the trees all its drumming light, full
and moving, a stratagem that dawn
throws no light on. After the moon, only
a lull.

> "... how everything turns away / Quite leisurely ...."

—W. H. Auden

The island steams under the opening sky.
All around the narrow length of land
the river flows as it always has, and late

birds heading north to Canada notice
nothing unusual about the air.
There may, or may not, have been a disaster

among the undergrowth: what birds may tell
is augured late at best, and fish homing
upstream are mainly interested in falls.

Who knows? At any rate the land was calm.
Nothing surprised farmers off their tractors
or knocked the rheumy cattle off their hoofs,

though something surely must disappear every
time the earth shakes or the sky moves an inch
or two to right or left. Still there will always

be a boy fishing from some river bank
who doesn't especially want anything to happen
except summer and a dog scratching at his side.

During the war
we drew all our troops to us.

We reveled in our reality
of wrong, marched miles across

littered plains, bridged chasms
hell could not imagine.

There was an art
to our displacement of men.

We leveled towns.
Territory was our game;

to take and hold,
our order and our last command.

Too small,
we could not think a Buchenwald:

not once
did we save one Jew.

Now forty odd years past,
I go back to that scored hill of dirt,

taking our whole battleground
in three strides—

the fortifications barely discernible,
the roads merely passable.

What scars we left
grow invisible:

the turbulent grass
is climbing toward the light,

though at the roots
I hear a drumming of small lost things.

Mostly I recall that blue bust of him
she hugged into my shop before they took
her off, though I remember, other times,
the odd anguish in her face as she held
on to her man's gone arm at this counter,
his drunken logger's idiocies branding
him fool the rest of his short staggered days.

Cancer took him and ravaged her insane.
Duty to the ghost of that poor woman
holds back all indecencies. What matter
the battered kids and broken rosary?
What I remember most is I knew she
suffered and loved, true to her deep devotion
to the fool. She pawned that blue legacy, too.
I gave her what I thought I could, and more.

I don't sleep well. Heart, you know. I knew him
when art failed him, or he his art. Who knows
genius? He bragged about his work in fir
and hemlock. And sold none. Winters he said
he burned his best work to stay alive. I
have hated myself, mea culpa, many
a night: I often see that simple piece
she painted blue. Don't ask why. I'm ashamed
to have taken her last token of his art.

Now, surely, somewhere in the green reaches
of loggerdoom, her mad sculptor unlimps
and lugs his chainsaw deep into timber,
decking a tall heaven full of angels
and grace. There in blue light she waits, his stew
steaming over pitch, coffee in the pot.

I've kept it out of greed: I longed to hold
what was left of the poor art and artist,
something I'd never get from the watches,
music boxes, old coats, lies. I have it
here, under the tarp, the odd and the end.
It is yours. Consider the clarity
of pain, the total blue. You may wish to
remove the paint. It is permissible.
I know the wood is blue: it must be blue.

Where Fourche Maline runs into Holson Creek,
first it almost does then backs off and makes
a circle so that an almost island
sits as though the river's god forgot his job.
Corn was growing on the hump when I was too
young to gnaw an ear. Now it has faded
back to forest, or just about: river
birches stand thick as cockleburs once choked
corn. It smells of musk and old earth where I
kick a last flood's log and turn up a black
twoheaded stone axe and a gunning sound of quail.
I'm too vague to care: my head is too full
of generalities. I cannot think
this a field of corn. How can I reach
Caddoes or pre-Columbians said to
have lived this land? I came to fish but think
of paying rent, the way it has to be.
I take the axe, just in case it charges
me with the fire it may have felt.

                              The line
hangs straight into the stream and bends. A minute
on my butt and I drift. The current's vague.
After rent then what's left? That blonde I saw
the other day showed me my age: cold fish
eye. Why I came back I will never know.
Fox squirrels killed here have no grave where I
can kneel, and bass never bite when the sign
is in the groin. Call it a try at going
with the sun.

            I tell the wife I want to get
away: a needed rest. But not from her,
I lie. Going I know I'm free, but that's
another lie. Earth never is the same.
I remember cornfields, but find a forest
and an axe. The field once I ran across,
lister rows thick with river grass: here is
another world. One I don't know and don't
care to. My work is with the real. But how
to live? I make mine eight to five and see
the joke. A stone axe in my hand is cold
comfort. Crumbling, it's hardly worth the trip.

(Carson & Barnes)

The artists are tired, tired: the sky has fallen
from their faces. A triple turns into
a flop. Even the net is slow in rebound.
The flyers' arc lacks the majesty of apes.
The catcalls of wild children rip the tent.

Clowns out of round empty their buckets on
rows one and two. No one flinches at
confetti: the trick is slower than the mind.
No one wants balloons that will not rise or
cotton candy elephants have disclaimed.

The cats refuse the flaming loops. The tamer
cracks his slow whip on empty air: the lions
will not wake, and the toothless tiger chews
a wrong memory of home. Not one cat couchant
or fierce enough to open the midget's mouth.

The jugglers lose their pins. Knees buckle
on the wire: the drop, a deadly 3-foot-6.
The spinner cannot spin by teeth alone
and begs the spectators to let her have
her hands, hung heavy with the brass of rings.

And now the grand promenade. The brilliant flash
of tights and eyes is gone. The heavy weight
of hoofs, a precise funeral march, brings all
performers down to earth, their final show,
to bow at last in a dangerous company of beasts.

Jim Barnes is the author of *The Fish on Poteau Mountain*
(1980) and *The American Book of the Dead* (1982). In 1980 he
was awarded a translation prize by Columbia University for
his translation *Summons and Sign: Poems by Dagmar Nick*.
Presently, he is editor of *The Chariton Review* and associate
professor of comparative literature at Northeast Missouri
State University. His Choctaw-Welsh-English heritage
colors his work, which has been published in *Carriers of the
Dream Wheel: Contemporary Native American Poetry*, *The Na-
tion*, *Missouri Review*, *Mundus Artium*, and *Georgia Review*,
among many other magazines and anthologies.

More poetry from Purdue

All That So Simple

Neil Myers

" . . . a tribute to the power that rhythm and a sense of language-as-music can give poetry."—James Moore

"[He] writes with such artistry that whatever he presents us with appears in its essence."—Arturo Vivante

72 pages, illustrated, ISBN 0-911198-56-3, $4.00

The Artist and the Crow

Dan Stryk

"[His] poems are grounded in his effortless and strict voice. And his voice is an eye. . . . a fine and welcome collection."—William Heyen

"A reader finds landscapes or settings, and their inhabitants, that come alive in richly textured but unvaryingly precise language."—Ralph J. Mills, Jr.

96 pages, illustrated, ISBN 0-911198-71-7, $5.25